THOMAS PLANT

BCP1662

THE PRAYER BOOK SOCIETY TEEN GUIDE TO THE BOOK OF COMMON PRAYER

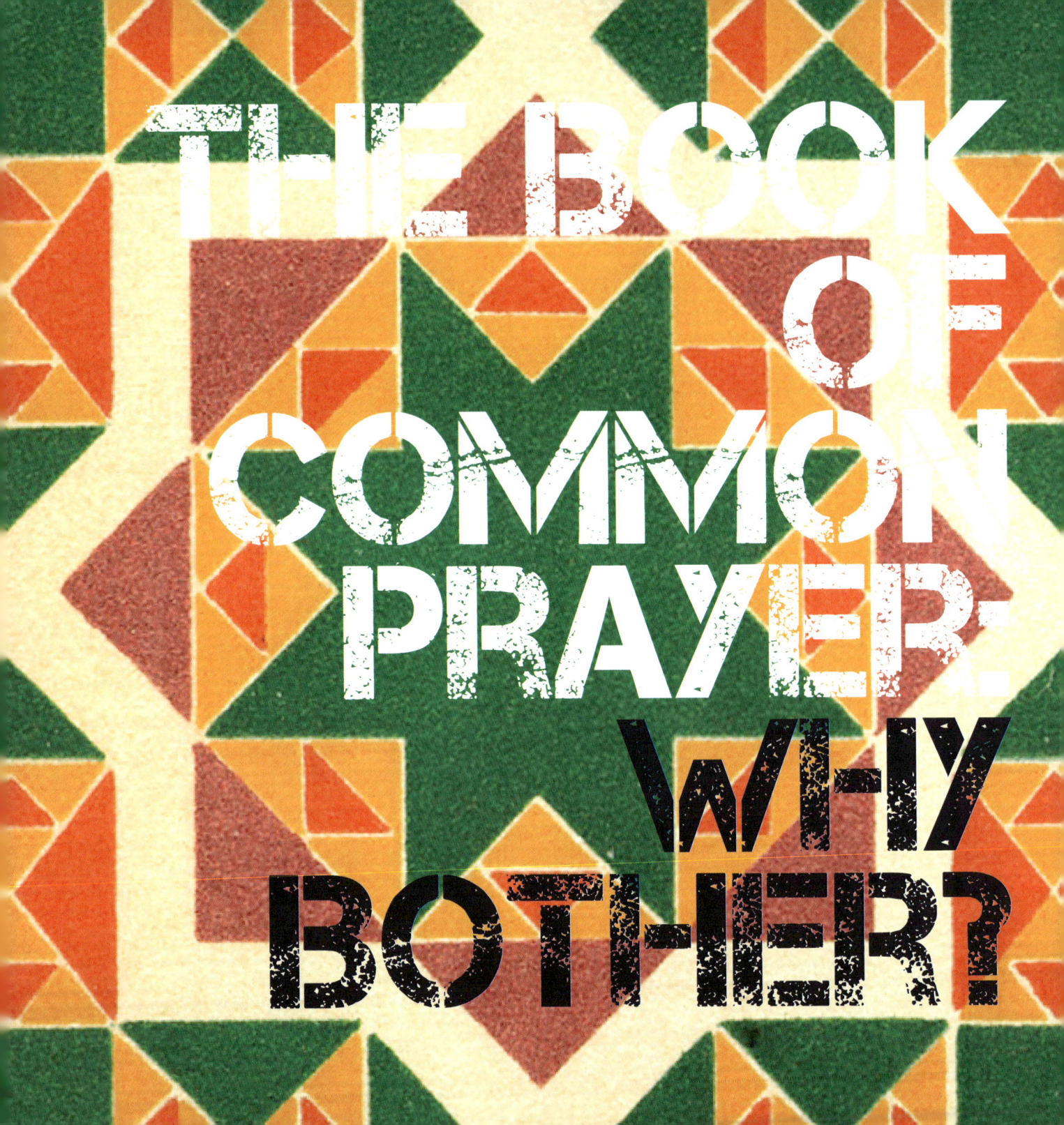

TOP FIVE REASONS TO USE THE BCP

1 Sound teaching If you want to know what the Church of England teaches, the BCP is your one-stop place to find it. Yes, some of the teaching has been updated and reinterpreted since 1662, but the Prayer Book is still the second authority for the English Church after the Bible, and the best place to start understanding the Anglican way.

2 Easy to use The BCP and the Bible are all you need for every service, from Holy Communion and Daily Prayer through to weddings and funerals. No libraries of texts or sprawling websites are needed.

3 Beautiful language The words of the Prayer Book are memorable. The poetic beauty of the texts helps to lift the soul to God. It may be old language, but if Muslims can learn Arabic and Jews can learn Hebrew, then English Christians should manage Elizabethan English!

4 Literary heritage After the King James Bible and Shakespeare, there is no greater influence on English literature than the Book of Common Prayer. If you don't know your Prayer Book, your understanding of centuries of English philosophy, poetry, plays and novels will be very limited.

5 English tradition This is the book used by our grandparents, their parents, their parents' parents and so on, all the way back to the 16th century — and it is built on the even older Catholic tradition of the pre-Reformation Church. The Prayer Book connects us with our ancestors in the faith.

YOUR SPIRITUAL TOOLKIT

If you've ever tried making anything, you'll know how hard it is without decent tools. You won't cut much wood with a blunt saw.

You need the right tools, too. It's no use trying to cut a pizza with a hacksaw, or a log with a pizza-cutter. Or pick your teeth with a chainsaw.

Then, you've got to know where your tools are. Otherwise, by the time you find them it might be too late. They need to be kept tidy, well-arranged so that you can quickly find the right one for the job. A bit like your bedroom...

And if you're on the move, you need a good box to keep them in, all in one place and easy to carry around.

This book is an introduction to the toolkit for your soul.

The tools this kit contains are of the highest quality, so high that they have lasted almost 500 years. The English Church has been using them since 1549, and they still are every bit as sharp as they were back then.

There is a different tool for each of your spiritual needs, some for building anew and others for ongoing maintenance: tools for making a new Christian, tools for strengthening the faith, tools for servicing the soul and running your spiritual MOT.

The tools are well ordered, and once you know where to look, you will never have trouble finding them. The order may seem strange at first, but this book will help you to make sense of why they are where they are.

Best of all, these tools are mobile, all contained in one neat little toolbox. You don't need an entire van to carry them, because this toolkit is small enough to fit into your pocket.

The toolkit is called the Book of Common Prayer.

"Once upon a time, there was a bad old king called Henry VIII who wanted a divorce, and so he broke away from the Catholic Church and set up a new one to get what he wanted."

Or so the story goes. But it's not quite true.

Now, King Henry VIII may well have been a bad old king — some would say he was an absolute monster — but a divorce is not technically what he was after. He wanted his marriage to Queen Catherine "annulled": that is, for the Church to say that it had never really been valid in the first place. Why? Because none of his male children, who would be heirs to the throne, had survived – and he started to think that this was a punishment from God for marrying his dead brother's wife, which was forbidden in the Bible. This may sound strange to our modern ears, but in the sixteenth century, people took these things very seriously indeed. And after all, the Pope had granted other monarchs annulments of their marriages on far weaker grounds, so why should he not help Henry?

The answer to this question is as much about politics as it is about religion (in fact, in those days, you could not really separate the two).

You see, Queen Catherine had a very powerful nephew: none other than the Holy Roman Emperor, Charles V. The Pope relied on Charles V and was hardly going to go against him by granting Henry his annulment.

Henry VIII was a very loyal Catholic, but he did not see why the Pope, Bishop of Rome, should have such a political influence in England. This is why he started the process of separating the English Church from the Roman Catholic Church. He did not mean to start a new Protestant church, but rather to have the English part of the Catholic Church ruled by the English king, under English law.

This is where the story of the Book of Common Prayer begins.

Its origins may not be very promising, but anyone who looks to the Cross of Christ knows that God can make good things come even out of the worst situations.

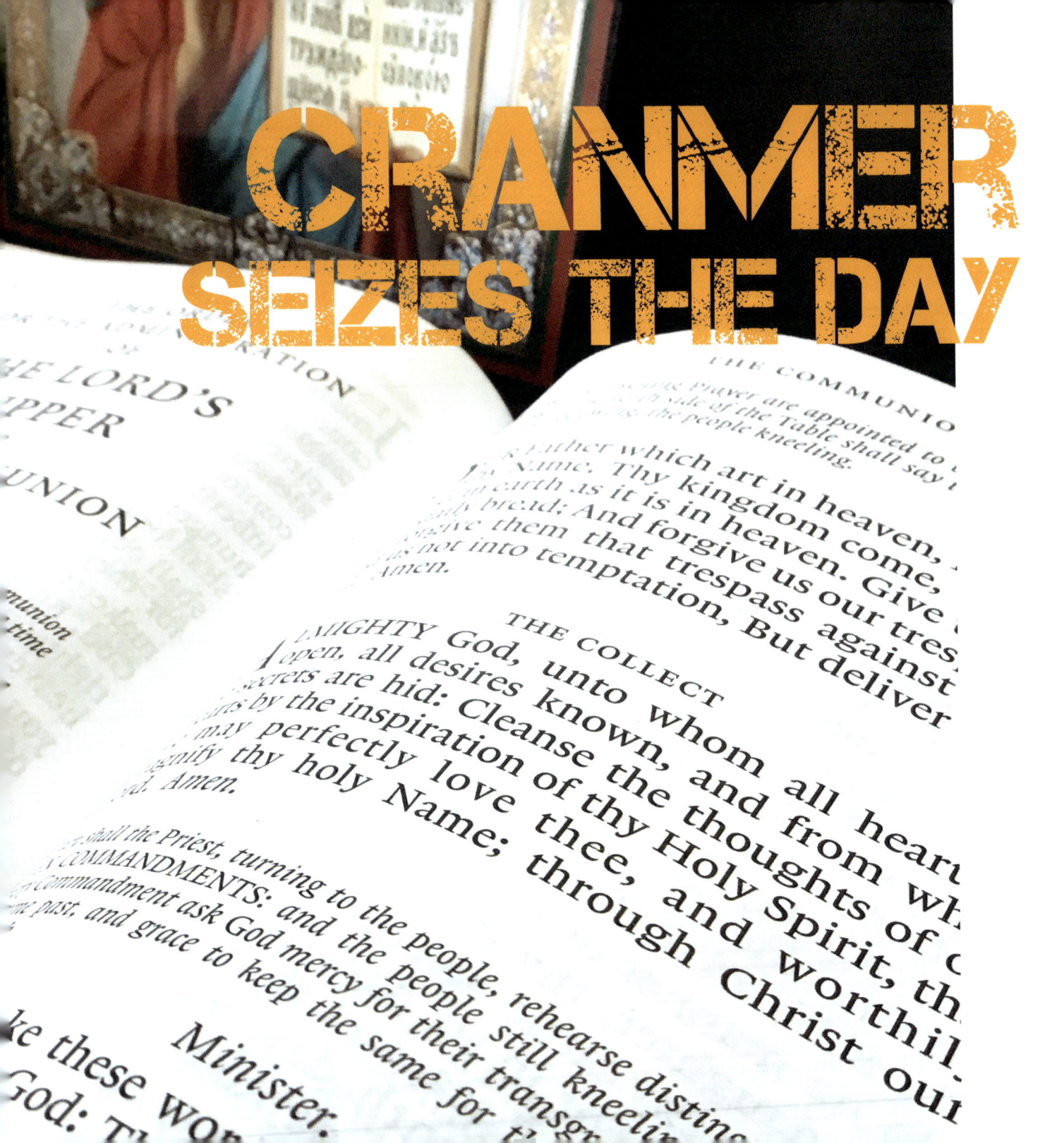

CRANMER SEIZES THE DAY

Henry needed someone loyal to help him make the break from Rome, and Thomas Cranmer was the man he chose, appointing him in 1532 as the highest bishop in the land: the Archbishop of Canterbury.

Henry himself was not all that interested in the new religious ideas of Protestantism which were getting fashionable in Europe; but Cranmer was. In particular, he thought that the English people should be able to worship God in the English language. At the time, people were being executed even for translating the Bible into their own languages. All services were in Latin, and the Bible was read only in Latin.

People did understand a lot of what was going on through performances of Bible stories called "mystery plays," through preaching, and through the paintings and statues in churches, but there was a lot more that they simply could not understand because it was being said in an ancient language. Certainly, most people could not read a bible or understand what the priests were saying in services. Often, even the priests themselves did not understand what they were saying.

Cranmer also found that you needed dozens of books just to carry out the usual daily services: so much so, he said, that you might spend more time looking for the right page than actually praying and worshipping.

His thought about the Christian faith was also influenced by the new "Reformers," such as Martin Luther and John Calvin, whose ideas were sweeping Europe. The Reformers thought that the Church had changed too much since its earliest days, and wanted to take it back to how they thought it should be. Whether or not they got it right is another question, but at least, that is what they were trying to do.

For Cranmer, Henry's break from Rome was an opportunity to reform the Church in England: not to form a new church, but to take the great treasures of the past, remove what he thought were later additions and corruptions, and put it into the language which the English people could hear, read and understand. He wanted to translate the old Latin texts and services, trim them down, and rearrange them into just one book. A book which everybody would have in "common:" one book for the whole English church.

So, in 1549, two years after Henry VIII died, Cranmer published the first Book of Common Prayer.

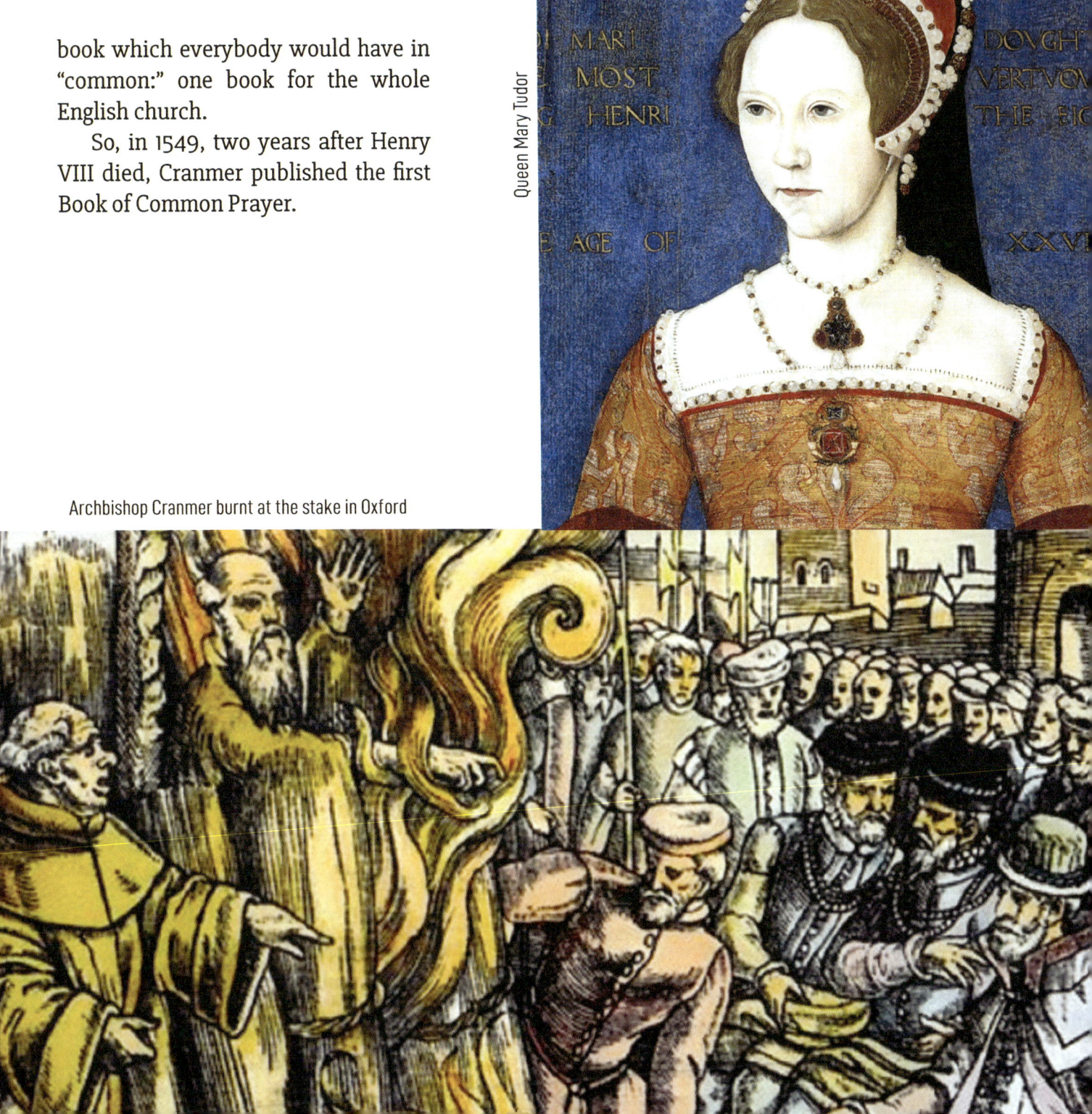

Queen Mary Tudor

Archbishop Cranmer burnt at the stake in Oxford

A BOOK TO DIE FOR?

Cranmer wanted every church in the country to have an English bible and a Book of Common Prayer. This was not always popular at first. Many people did not like the change or the way it was being imposed on them from on high. They wanted to keep the old ways.

It did not help when the new King, young Edward VI, introduced a new edition of the Book of Common Prayer in 1552 which was more radically reformed than the 1549 original. By this time, Cranmer was much more strongly influenced by the Protestant movements of Europe. So when Edward died young, at the age of 15, and (after a nine-day interval) was succeeded by the Catholic Queen Mary, many of the people were happy to see the new prayer books burned and the Roman Catholic services restored. They were less happy, though, when Mary burned Protestant people along with their books: at least 300 men and women in all.

On 21 March 1556, in Oxford, Archbishop Cranmer was one of them.

Although Cranmer died, his Book of Common Prayer did not die with him. Mary's reign lasted only five years, and her successor, Queen Elizabeth I, revived his work. She wanted an English church in which those of more Protestant and Catholic views could worship and work together. She was not entirely successful in this, and she did persecute Catholics who would not submit to the authority of the English church. Her hands were not clean of blood. And yet, through the Book of Common Prayer, she did manage to contain some of the disagreements and arguments between Christians and keep the English church as one.

The next major edition of the Book of Common Prayer would come one hundred years later. King Charles I was under pressure from more extreme Protestants in Parliament to take the Reformation much further. They wanted him to abandon much of the ancient tradition contained in the Book of Common Prayer. Especially, though, they wanted the King to abolish the "Episcopate," the ancient order of Bishops, whom the Church believes to be the direct descendants of the Apostles whom Jesus chose himself. Civil war ensued and the King was executed.

For eleven years, the country was ruled as a republic by Puritans, extreme Protestants. Oliver Cromwell ruled as Lord Protector from 1652 to 1658. Kings were banned, bishops were banned — and the Prayer Book was banned. Only when the monarchy was restored in 1660 under Charles II could it be brought back into use.

By this time, the Prayer Book had been in use for over a hundred years, and instead of being seen as something new and radical, people thought of it as very traditional. The Puritans who had ruled the country for eleven years thought that the Reformation had not gone far enough, and the Prayer Book was "too Catholic." King Charles II

The execution of King Charles I, Saint and Martyr

needed to keep peace with them, and so called a conference between the Puritans and the newly-restored bishops to discuss a new edition of the Prayer Book. In fact, very few of the Puritans' objections were upheld, and the bishops managed to make some changes which took the Prayer Book somewhat closer to its original, more "Catholic" 1549 form.

The bishops published their new edition in 1662, and this is the Prayer Book we still have, almost unchanged, to this day: the 1662 Book of Common Prayer.

The Contents of this BOOK.

1. THE Acts for the Uniformity of Common Prayer.
2. The Preface.
3. Concerning the Service of the Church.
4. Concerning Ceremonies.
5. The Order how the Psalter is appointed to be read.
6. The Order how the rest of the Holy Scripture is appointed to be read.
7. A Table of Proper Lessons and Psalms.
8. Tables and Rules for the Feasts and Fasts throughout the whole Year.
9. The Kalendar, with the Table of Lessons.
10. The Order for Morning Prayer.
11. The Order for Evening Prayer.
12. The Creed of Saint *Athanasius*.
13. The Litany.
14. Prayers and Thanksgivings upon several Occasions.
15. The Collects, Epistles and Gospels, to be used at the Ministration of the holy Communion throughout the Year.
16. The Order of the Ministration of the Holy Communion.
17. The Order of Baptism, both Publick and Private.
18. The Order of Baptism for [...] per Years.
19. The Catechism, with the [Con]firmation of Children.
20. The Form of Solemnizati[on ...] mony.
21. Visitation of the Sick, and [...] the Sick.
22. The Order for the Burial [...]
23. Thanksgiving for Wome[n ...] bearing.
24. A Commination, or Deno[uncing] Anger and Judgments [...] ners.
25. The Psalter.
26. The Order of Prayers to [...] Sea.
27. A Form of Prayer with Tha[nksgiving] the Fifth Day of *November*.
28. A Form of Prayer with Fa[sting] Thirtieth Day of *January*.
29. A Form of Prayer with [...] for the Nine and twentie[th ...] *May*.
30. A Form of Prayer with Tha[nksgiving] the Eleventh Day of *June*.

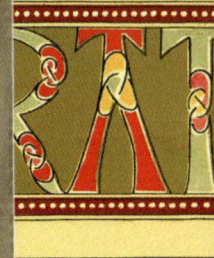

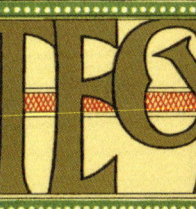

WHAT'S INSIDE?

We know where our spiritual toolkit has come from. So now, it's time to look inside.

At first glance, the contents may not make much sense. But think back to the Prayer Book's history, and what Cranmer was trying to do. He was taking a whole library of books which were needed for all the services of the church year and putting them together into one. Behind our English Prayer Book lies a vast tradition of ancient Latin liturgy and prayer.

In Cranmer's day, to run church services, you needed at least five books —>

> The **Breviary** was used by monks, nuns and priests for praying the "Daily Office" or "Liturgy of the Hours," at least five services of Psalms and Bible readings at set times each day.

> The **Processional** was a slim volume of set prayers called "litanies" which would be chanted in processions.

> The **Missal** contained the order for the Mass, also called the Eucharist or Holy Communion, for each day of the year.

> The **Manual** contained other services, including baptism, marriage, funerals and so on.

> The **Pontifical** was a special book for bishops, including the rites for ordaining new priests and deacons, and also Confirmation.

FIVE BOOKS IN ONE

Cranmer took these five books and condensed them down into one. So, here are the tools in the box:

1 The Calendar, showing all the feast days and saints' days of the year, with the "lessons" (readings) for every day, and the two daily services of Morning and Evening Prayer replaced the Breviary. This was so that not just priests, monks and nuns, but everybody could join in with the Daily Office. What's more, Cranmer spread out the readings so that everyone would read the whole Bible once each year.

2 A single Litany replaced the Processional. This is read or sung on certain days after the Daily Office, and so that is where Cranmer put it.

3 The Collects, Epistles and Gospels and the Order of Ministration of the Holy Communion replaced the Missal. The order for Communion is at the centre of the Book of Common Prayer for both a symbolic and a practical reason:

Symbolically, Communion is at the heart of the Christian life of prayer. In Cranmer's day, most Christians received Communion only two or three times each year. Cranmer wanted Communion to be celebrated every week, which is why he provides prayers (Collects) and readings (Epistles and Gospels) for every week and every major feast day of the year.

Practically, the Priest needs the book to stay open when celebrating Communion, and so the middle of the book is the best place to avoid the pages flicking shut half way through the service.

4 The orders for Baptism, Confirmation, Matrimony (marriage), Visitation of the Sick and Burial of the Dead replace the Manual, and are in a very logical order, taking the Christian from the beginning right to the end of life.

Cranmer also very logically put the Catechism in between Baptism and Confirmation. The Catechism is a Q&A about the Christian faith which Confirmation candidates were expected to learn off by heart. The Bishop would test them on the questions before agreeing to confirm them.

The Psalter is the next major section of the Prayer Book, and contains all of the Psalms in order, set out for reading daily. Cranmer wanted the people to use this at Morning and Evening Prayer, so that they would read all the Psalms every month.

5 Finally, the Form and Manner of Making, Ordaining, and Consecrating of Bishops, Priests and Deacons replaced the Pontifical. The Church of England has always kept the three ancient orders of ministry of the one Catholic Church, and the Prayer Book has guarded this tradition. "Vicar" is a title given to the priest who is responsible for a parish, though often the Prayer Book refers to the vicar as "Curate".

All you need for every service in the Church year and for every stage of the Christian life is the Prayer Book and a Bible.

(You might want a hymn book, too, but you get the point.)

THE BCP USER'S GUIDE

We've got our tools. We've checked their quality and looked into their maker. We've opened the box and looked inside, worked out how they are stored and ordered. Now all we need to know is how to use them.

This requires some skill. But then, isn't that true of any tools? Even the best tools on the market won't be much use unless they are in the hands of a skilled craftsman.

Let's learn our trade. Remember that the work in question is building and maintaining the soul. An important task. But happily, many generations have gone before us to show us the way: saints and sages, certainly, but also everyday, ordinary people who for centuries have toiled at the spirit with the Prayer Book in their hands and its words on their lips.

So, the first thing to realise is that while you can use many of these tools on your own, they are really designed to be used as part of a team. Praying at home on your own is part of the Christian life, but only part. The basic building block of our spiritual edifice is this: going to church.

Right, you may be thinking. Why would I want to do that? Do I really want to commit my Sunday mornings to hanging out with a bunch of old duffers and people I'm really not all that interested in?

Actually, that's part of the point.

Remember that we are talking about the Book of Common Prayer: that is, prayer for everybody, whoever they may be.

Young and old, women and men, rich and poor: the Prayer Book is written for us all, not just for "people like me."

HOLY COMMUNION

Holy Communion is the firm foundation for our spiritual building. The Book of Common Prayer expects us to take part every Sunday: to hear the Gospel, that is the good news of Jesus Christ, and to receive the sacrament of his Body and his Blood.

In Baptism, says the Catechism, we are given "death unto sin" and "new birth unto righteousness." Throughout our life, Holy Communion then gives us "strengthening and refreshing of our souls" so that we may "be in charity with all men": that is, live in love with all people.

If we think that we can do this without Communion, then we are mistaken. You only need to look around the world to see just how badly we humans do when we rely on ourselves, and how much we need God's grace. Holy Communion is the food for our souls by which God gives us his grace.

To attend Holy Communion with skill, we need to make sure that we have confessed what we have done wrong (our sins) to God beforehand, so that we receive the full measure of his forgiveness. This can be done privately in prayer on your own, and you might use the material at the beginning of Morning and Evening Prayer to help you.

If something is especially weighing on your conscience, the Prayer Book makes provision for one-to-one confession with a priest.

The order for this is detailed under the Visitation of the Sick, another handy tool from the kit. It doesn't have to be particularly formal, and many people find it a great spiritual benefit.

The Lichfield Icon: blood and water stream from Christ's side, so water and wine are mixed in the chalice at Communion

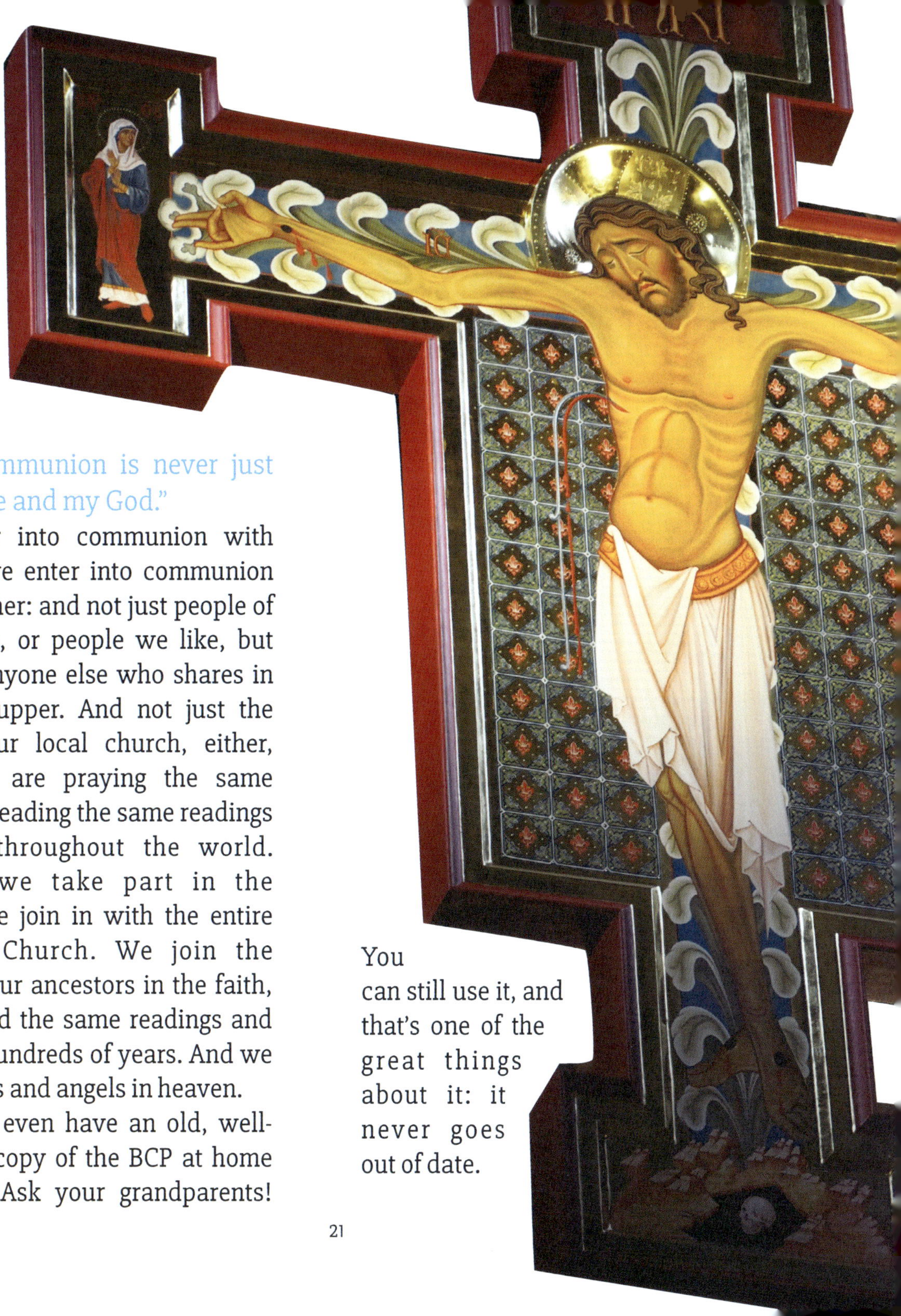

Holy Communion is never just between "me and my God."

We enter into communion with God while we enter into communion with each other: and not just people of our own age, or people we like, but absolutely anyone else who shares in the Lord's Supper. And not just the people in our local church, either, because we are praying the same prayers and reading the same readings as people throughout the world. Whenever we take part in the Eucharist, we join in with the entire worldwide Church. We join the tradition of our ancestors in the faith, too, who used the same readings and prayers for hundreds of years. And we join the saints and angels in heaven.

You may even have an old, well-used family copy of the BCP at home somewhere. Ask your grandparents! You can still use it, and that's one of the great things about it: it never goes out of date.

COLLECT, EPISTLE, GOSPEL

The tools we will need to lay the foundation of Holy Communion are the Collect, Epistle and Gospel for the Sunday, towards the middle of the Prayer Book.

"Epistle" comes from the Greek word for "letter," and will be taken from one of the many letters in the New Testament.

The Gospel, meaning "good news," is a story about Jesus or some of his own words, taken from one of his four biblical biographies.

Both readings will be used at the Sunday celebration of Holy Communion, and often for celebrations later in the same week.

With this page marked, we then turn to the order for Holy Communion and follow the service through, turning to the Collect and readings when we need them.

But the Collect (stress on the first syllable!) is a multi-purpose tool. We will use it not only for Holy Communion, but also at Morning and Evening Prayer every day. You get even more use out of the collects for Advent and Ash Wednesday, as these are used not just for a week, but for an entire season of the Church year.

The Collects were not made up by Cranmer: they are mostly translations of ancient Latin prayers. They connect us all the way back to the tradition of the early Church.

Nor are they random. Cranmer carefully chose each Collect to match up with the Epistle and Gospel reading for the week. When you read a Collect, see if you can work out the connection with the readings, as this will make it a much more meaningful prayer for you. It is like a spiritual key to the meaning of the texts.

< "Lord, hear my prayer, and let my cry come unto Thee." Psalm 102

The Archangel Michael, leader of the heavenly armies who pray with us

MORNING AND EVENING PRAYER

So far, we have laid the foundations of our spiritual life by joining in Holy Communion each Sunday. Many people are happy to leave things there; but the Prayer Book system gives us the tools to build on those foundations, little by little, day by day. These are the "Daily Office" of Morning and Evening Prayer.

Every Bishop, Priest and Deacon in the Church of England is obliged to ring the bell and pray Morning and Evening Prayer in church every day. But Cranmer's hope was that everybody, not just the clergy, would be able to join in this great daily cycle of prayer. You can join in at church, if you have the time, and in some churches (especially cathedrals), you may find that one or other of these offices is sung by a choir — in which name the services tend to be called "Mattins" and "Evensong."

For most people, getting to church before and after work every single day is not practical, but there is no reason why we cannot pray the Daily Office on our own. It's just a matter of making the time each morning and evening — or just one of the two, if that's all the time you have. You can also shorten the Office if you need to.

So, let's make a start. You will need a Prayer Book, a Bible and some bookmarks or ribbons.

First, you look up the readings in the Calendar at the beginning of the Prayer Book and mark your places in the Bible. There will be one reading from the Old Testament and one from the New. If you only have time for one reading, then so be it! But if you do manage to follow the table of lessons, you will read the entire Bible once each year, as Cranmer intended.

Next, you mark the Psalms of the day. These are towards the back of the Prayer Book, set out for the morning and evening of each day of the month. Again, you may need to cut down to just one of the Psalms if time is short.

You will also need to mark the Collect, the special prayer for the week, ready for use at the end of your prayers. These you will find towards the middle of the Prayer Book, with the Epistles and Gospels — but you know that already.

Now you turn to Morning or Evening Prayer and follow it through.

Praying the Daily Office can be confusing at first because of the optional canticles, but the basic pattern is this:

Morning Prayer
- Penitential material (optional)
- Opening versicle: O Lord, open thou our lips
- Opening canticle: Psalm 95
- Psalms from the Psalter
- Old Testament Reading
- Te Deum (Song of St Ambrose)
- New Testament Reading
- Benedictus (Song of Zechariah)
- Creed and prayers, finishing with the Collects

Evening Prayer
- Penitential material (optional)
- Opening versicle: O Lord, open thou our lips
- Psalms from the Psalter
- Old Testament Reading
- Magnificat (Song of Mary)
- New Testament Reading
- Nunc Dimittis (Song of Simeon)
- Creed and prayers, finishing with the Collects

For a quicker version, you can cut out the penitential material and try the follIIowing:

Short Morning Prayer
- Opening versicle: O Lord, open thou our lips
- Opening canticle: Ps 95
- Psalms from the Psalter
- One Bible Reading
- Benedictus (Song of Zechariah)
- Creed and prayers, finishing with the Collects

Short Evening Prayer
- Opening versicle: O Lord, open thou our lips
- Psalms from the Psalter
- One Bible Reading
- Magnificat (Song of Mary)
- Creed and prayers, finishing with the Collects

If this defeats you, fear not! There is a Daily Prayer app on iOS and Android. Or, to save flicking through pages, you can also find the Daily Office online at:

bit.ly/1662DailyOffice

THE BIG THREE...

...AND THE REST

The Prayer Book toolkit is quite a lot simpler than it first looks. We have seen the three main tools it contains:

1 The Order of Baptism, which can be received only once in a lifetime, for the washing away of sins and for new birth to righteousness;

2 The Holy Communion, for the frequent refreshing and strengthening of our souls;

3 The Daily Office, for the constant reading of Scripture and daily growth in our relationship with God.

There are plenty of other tools in the kit, for each part of your life.

For teenagers, perhaps the next most relevant one is the Order of Confirmation and the Catechism which leads up to it. If you want to learn more about the Christian faith as it is understood in the Church of England, the Catechism is an excellent place to start. It will hone your skills with all of the tools the Prayer Book contains.

With God helping you and inspiring you through the time-tested words of the Book of Common Prayer, who knows what a great temple for the Lord you might build?

Thank you for buying this book. If you have enjoyed it, please leave a review on Amazon, where you can buy these books, too!

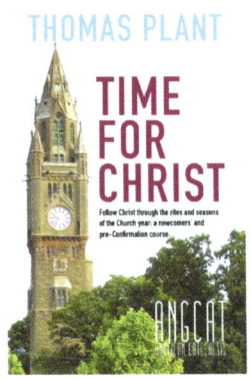

If you are considering Confirmation or would like to learn more about the Church year and her liturgy, try Time for Christ, new in 2019.

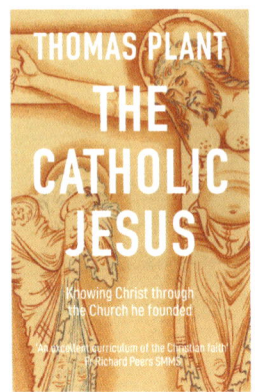

Who was Jesus? Just some liberal rabbi, or more? Did he really think he was God? What does he have to do with the Church? The Catholic Jesus is ideal for the A-Level Religious Studies specification on the person of Christ, and for general reading.

Want to learn how to pray? Looking for some discipline in organising your spiritual life? This prayer diary gives monthly and weekly pages for you to fill in with people and causes that need your prayers, along with advice and traditional prayers from the BCP.

For the author's blog and details of new releases, please visit
www.greatersilence.com

Printed in Poland
by Amazon Fulfillment
Poland Sp. z o.o., Wrocław